D0759737

TABLE OF
CONTENTS

A DOGSLED RIDE

MUSHER

DOGSLED

A thick layer of snow covers the ground at the edge of a forest. Six Siberian huskies jump around their musher, or driver, in excitement. The musher places harnesses on the dogs and climbs onto the back of the dogsled. Everyone is ready. Mush!

SIBERIAN HUSKY

SNOW HEROES

In the winter of 1925, a deadly disease called diphtheria struck many people in Nome, Alaska. Twenty teams of sled dogs crossed 674 miles (1,085 kilometers) to bring medicine to the town.

The dogs speed through the forest as the musher calls directions. Long ago, dogs pulled sleds to move people and goods across snowy land. Today, the musher and his Siberian huskies are riding for fun!

THE WORKING GROUP

SAMOYED

SAMOYED SMILE

Samoyeds have lips that curl up at the corners. Many people think this looks like a smile!

The working group is a group of dog breeds joined together by the American Kennel Club, or AKC. The group was created in 1924. There were fewer than 10 working breeds at that time. Many breeds have been added since.

Dogs in the working group are known for their history of helping humans. Some breeds are very old. The Samoyed and the kuvasz have been at work for more than 1,000 years. Other breeds are newer. The Dogo Argentino was **bred** in the 1920s. It joined the working group in 2020!

DOGO ARGENTINO

TOP 5 WORKING DOGS

1 **ROTTWEILER**

2 **BOXER**

3 **SIBERIAN HUSKY**

4 **GREAT DANE**

5 **DOBERMAN PINSCHER**

Today, 31 breeds make up the working group. They were bred to perform a wide range of jobs. Many of the oldest breeds guarded livestock or property. The Great Pyrenees has chased wolves away from sheep for centuries. Hunting was another important activity. Great Danes and Cani Corsi began as hunters more than 1,000 years ago!

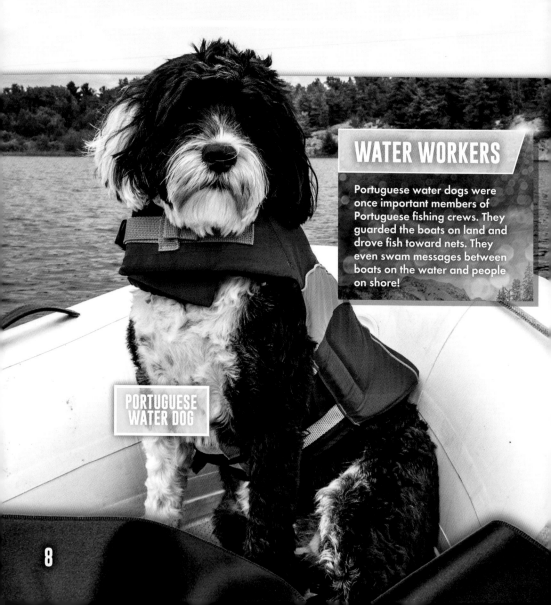

WATER WORKERS

Portuguese water dogs were once important members of Portuguese fishing crews. They guarded the boats on land and drove fish toward nets. They even swam messages between boats on the water and people on shore!

PORTUGUESE WATER DOG

WORKING GROUP CHAMPION

▶ **FULL NAME**
CINNIBON'S BEDROCK BOMBSHELL

▶ **NICKNAME**
WILMA

▶ **BREED**
BOXER

▶ **BIRTHDAY**
OCTOBER 8, 2015

▶ **TITLE**
WESTMINSTER KENNEL CLUB DOG SHOW BEST IN GROUP

▶ **YEAR WON**
2020

DOGUE DE BORDEAUX

Some dogs were bred to pull heavy loads. Dogues de Bordeaux are a **drafting** breed from France. Other breeds became known for pulling sleds through snow. **Hardy** sled dogs include Chinooks, Siberian huskies, Samoyeds, and Alaskan malamutes.

9

BERNESE
MOUNTAIN DOG

Most working dogs are large. The largest breeds, like Mastiffs, make great guard dogs. Bernese mountain dogs are another large breed. They have sturdy bodies that are perfect for drafting. Smaller breeds use their size to their advantage, too. German pinschers can squeeze into small spaces. They once helped farmers hunt rats!

Working dogs have many types of fur. Sled dogs were bred to have woolly undercoats. These helped the dogs stay warm in the snow. Waterproof coats protected Newfoundlands and Portuguese water dogs during water rescues. Corded coats gave komondorok camouflage. They could hide among the sheep to scare wolves away!

DOG SIZES

LARGEST BREED
MASTIFF

AVERAGE HEIGHT
30 INCHES
(76 CENTIMETERS)
AND UP

AVERAGE WEIGHT
120 TO 230 POUNDS
(54 TO 104 KILOGRAMS)

SMALLEST BREED
GERMAN PINSCHER

AVERAGE HEIGHT
17 TO 20 INCHES
(43 TO 51 CENTIMETERS)

AVERAGE WEIGHT
25 TO 45 POUNDS
(11 TO 20 KILOGRAMS)

Many working group breeds are known for being smart. The Chinook, Doberman pinscher, and Rottweiler are among the most intelligent. They are easily trained. Other breeds can be trained, too. These hardworking dogs learn to compete on agility courses or in drafting competitions.

DOBERMAN PINSCHER ON AN AGILITY COURSE

WORKING GROUP TRAITS

LARGE OR EXTRA-LARGE

LOYAL

PROTECTIVE

INTELLIGENT

STRONG

Guard dog breeds are alert and brave. They are loyal to their owners. These traits help them protect people, property, and livestock. Sled dogs tend to be more friendly and playful. These dogs have a lot of energy! They often enjoy being around people and other animals.

ROTTWEILER

WORKING DOGS AT WORK

GREAT PYRENEES

AKITA

Some working breeds continue to perform the tasks they were bred to do. Many breeds are known for their loyalty. This makes them excellent guard dogs. Akitas, bullmastiffs, and giant schnauzers are common guard dog breeds.

NEWFOUNDLAND
RESCUE DOG

Farmers use working dogs, too. Great Pyrenees and Anatolian shepherd dogs are two common farm breeds. These dogs protect goats, chickens, and other livestock. Newfoundlands are natural picks for search and rescue jobs on land and in water. Their strong sense of smell helps them track people in trouble. Webbed feet help these large, powerful swimmers with water rescues.

GREAT DANE
SERVICE DOG

SERVICE DOG

Many working breeds also succeed as service dogs. Boxers and Doberman pinschers are common guide dogs. While on the job, they assist people in safely performing everyday tasks. With training, Great Danes can become excellent partners for people with trouble moving around. Their strength, gentle nature, and giant size allow owners to safely walk and keep their balance.

Bernese mountain dogs and boerboels are known for their kind personalities. This makes them excellent therapy dogs. They visit schools, nursing homes, and hospitals to boost people's spirits!

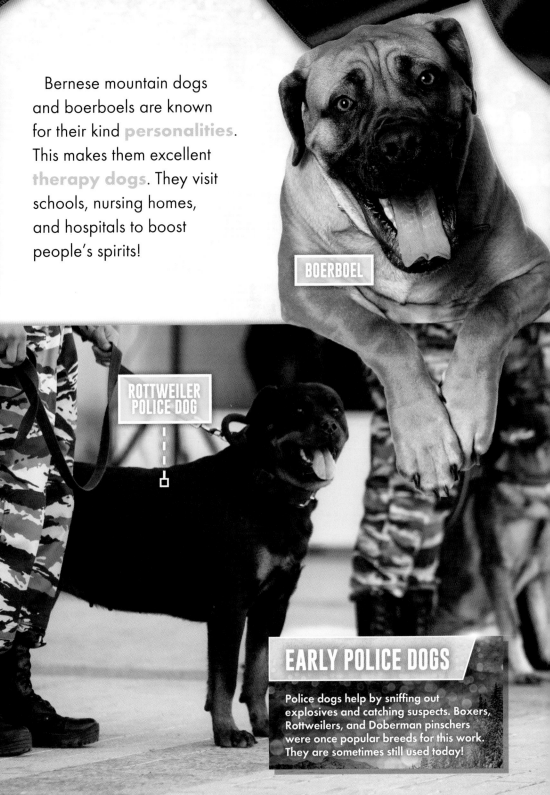

BOERBOEL

ROTTWEILER POLICE DOG

EARLY POLICE DOGS

Police dogs help by sniffing out explosives and catching suspects. Boxers, Rottweilers, and Doberman pinschers were once popular breeds for this work. They are sometimes still used today!

WORKING DOGS AS PETS

BOXER

Working group dogs make excellent pets. They can be loving, loyal, and playful with their families. Boxers and Bernese mountain dogs are popular picks for families with children.

Some dogs need more training from their owners. Breeds such as Siberian huskies and bullmastiffs are stubborn. Their large size can make them difficult to control. Akitas and kuvaszok do not always trust strangers. Owners must train them to be friendly. If trained properly, working dogs make great pets!

KUVASZOK

Many working breeds have a lot of energy. They need plenty of activity. Many owners take their dogs on hikes and runs. Some breeds enjoy swimming! Going on walks and playing fetch are also favorite activities. Exercise helps the dogs be happy and healthy!

GIANT SCHNAUZER

Some working dogs are trained to do dog sports. They can learn to race in tracking or herding trials. Most working dogs also enjoy agility courses. The working group is full of fun dog breeds!

ALASKAN MALAMUTE

DOBERMAN PINSCHER

Doberman pinschers are named for the first person to breed them, tax collector Louis Dobermann. In 1800s Germany, Dobermann needed a loyal dog to guard him while working. In time, Doberman pinschers became known as skilled guard dogs and police dogs. They even fought bravely alongside the U.S. Marine Corps in World War II!

DOBERMAN PINSCHER IN WORLD WAR II

PHYSICAL TRAITS

HEIGHT
24 to 28 inches
(61 to 71 centimeters)

WEIGHT
60 to 100 pounds
(27 to 45 kilograms)

PHYSICAL TRAITS
muscular body; short, smooth coat; pointed ears

LIFE SPAN
10 to 12 years

PERSONALITY
smart, protective, loyal

YEAR RECOGNIZED BY AKC
1908

COAT COLORS

BLACK AND RUST

BLUE AND RUST

FAWN AND RUST

RED AND RUST

SAINT BERNARD

Saint Bernards are famous for their rescue missions in the Swiss Alps. They were brought there by **monks** who used them to rescue travelers trapped in snow. The dogs' strong noses helped them sniff out people who had been buried by falling snow. They rescued about 2,000 people! By the 1800s, they arrived in the United States. The breed is still popular today!

PHYSICAL TRAITS

HEIGHT

26 to 30 inches
(66 to 76 centimeters)

WEIGHT

120 to 180 pounds
(54 to 82 kilograms)

PHYSICAL TRAITS

muscular body; large head;
thick coat

LIFE SPAN

8 to 10 years

PERSONALITY

alert, patient, curious

YEAR RECOGNIZED BY AKC

1885

COAT COLORS

BROWN
AND WHITE

MAHOGANY
AND WHITE

ORANGE
AND WHITE

SAMOYED

Samoyeds take their name from the Samoyede people of Siberia. This part of the world is very cold. The Samoyede people needed a dog that could handle freezing temperatures. They bred the Samoyed to hunt reindeer and pull sleds. In the 1700s, explorers brought the dogs to England. They quickly became popular!

PHYSICAL TRAITS

HEIGHT

19 to 23.5 inches
(48 to 60 centimeters)

WEIGHT

35 to 65 pounds
(16 to 29 kilograms)

PHYSICAL TRAITS

thick, fluffy fur; triangle-shaped
ears; fluffy tail

LIFE SPAN

12 to 14 years

PERSONALITY

smart, alert, friendly

YEAR RECOGNIZED BY AKC

1906

COAT COLORS

WHITE

CREAM

BISCUIT

ROTTWEILER

ROTTWEILER
MILITARY DOG

Rottweilers come from dogs used by the Roman Empire. The military needed strong, tough dogs to herd and guard cattle as soldiers marched. When the empire fell, these dogs were bred with other dogs in Germany. This led to the modern Rottweiler breed. Today, they often serve as police dogs, service dogs, and search and rescue dogs.

PHYSICAL TRAITS

HEIGHT
22 to 27 inches
(56 to 69 centimeters)

WEIGHT
80 to 135 pounds
(36 to 61 kilograms)

PHYSICAL TRAITS
muscular body; broad chest;
short, shiny coat

LIFE SPAN
9 to 10 years

PERSONALITY
calm, smart, protective

YEAR RECOGNIZED BY AKC
1931

COAT COLORS

BLACK AND MAHOGANY

BLACK AND RUST

BLACK AND TAN

GLOSSARY

agility—a sport in which dogs race to complete obstacle courses

alert—quick to notice or act

American Kennel Club—an organization that keeps track of dog breeds in the United States

bred—purposely mated to make puppies with certain qualities

breeds—types of dogs

camouflage—markings or coloring that help something to blend in with the surrounding environment

coats—the hair or fur covering some animals

drafting—used for hauling or pulling

hardy—tough and able to survive in harsh conditions

herding trials—competitions that test how well a dog can herd farm animals

intelligent—able to learn and be trained

loyal—having constant support for someone

monks—men who have devoted their lives to religion

personalities—the qualities that make living things different from one another

service dogs—dogs trained to help people who have special needs perform daily tasks

stubborn—difficult to train

therapy dogs—dogs trained to provide comfort and support to people

undercoats—thick layers of fur hidden by longer fur

TO LEARN MORE

AT THE LIBRARY

Gagne, Tammy. *Huskies, Mastiffs, and Other Working Dogs*. North Mankato, Minn.: Capstone Press, 2017.

Green, Sara. *Herding Dogs*. Minneapolis, Minn.: Bellwether Media, 2021.

Klepeis, Alicia Z. *Sled Racing Dogs*. Minneapolis, Minn.: Abdo Publishing, 2019.

ON THE WEB

FACTSURFER

Factsurfer.com gives you a safe, fun way to find more information.

1. Go to www.factsurfer.com.

2. Enter "working dogs" into the search box and click 🔍.

3. Select your book cover to see a list of related content.

INDEX